AURORA

A History in Pictures

YONGE ST.
AURORA ONT.

AURORA

A History in Pictures

by W. John McIntyre

THE BOSTON MILLS PRESS

Canadian Cataloguing in Publication Data

McIntyre, W. John (William John), 1951-
    Aurora: a history in pictures

Bibliography: p.
Includes index.
ISBN 0-919783-81-3

1. Aurora (Ont.) - History. 2. Aurora (Ont.) -
Description - Views. I. Title.

FC3099.A87M35 1988   971.3'547   C88-094324-6
F1059.5.A87M35 1988

Published by:
THE BOSTON MILLS PRESS
132 Main Street
Erin, Ontario N0B 1T0
(519) 833-2407
FAX: (519) 833-2195

American Association
for State and Local History
Award of Merit

Winners of the
Heritage Canada
Communications Award

Design by John Denison
Typography by Lexigraf, Tottenham
Printed by Ampersand, Guelph

We wish to acknowledge the encouragement and the financial
assistance of The Canada Council, the Ontario Arts Council
and the Office of the Secretary of State.

ACKNOWLEDGEMENTS

Most of the pictures chosen for this book have come from
the collections of the Aurora and District Historical Society at
the Aurora Museum. Listed below are the names of those who
donated these photographs to the Society along with the names
of people and institutions who have lent pictures from their
own collections:

Miss Bertha Andrews, Miss Marjorie Andrews, Archives of
Ontario, Town of Aurora, Aurora Heritage Committee, Mrs.
Ruth Bagshaw, Miss Margaret Belcher, Mrs. Pearl Borden, Miss
Helen Boynton, Mr. Cleon Bunn, Miss Rose Caruso, Miss Georgie
Charles, Miss Vera M. Clarke, Mr. Clarence Davis, Mr. Gary
Dawson, Dr. Audrey Devins, Mrs. Jean Dobbs, Dr. G.W. Williams
Secondary School, Mr. Albert Evans, Mrs. A. Gardhouse,
Miss Mildred H. Graham, Dr. E.J. Henderson, Miss E. Nora Hillary,
Mr. & Mrs. Horace Hillary, Mrs. Maude Hodgkinson, Mr.
Harry Holman, Mr. Roscoe Linton, Mrs. Lillian Lubbock, Markham
District Historical Museum, Mr. Donald C. McCallum, Mr.
Thomas M. McCammon, Mr. Edward McClenny, Mr. W. John
McIntyre, Mrs. William O. McIntyre, Mrs. Reita Moore, Mrs.
Alice Morris, Mrs. Dorothy Nisbet, T.H. Oliver Estate, Mr. R.C.
Osborne, Mrs. Elma Pinder, Miss Ruth Rothwell, Miss L.Z.
Sprague Estate, Mrs. H.C. Steels, Mr. William Stephens, Mrs.
Doris M.E. Thorp, Trinity Anglican Church, Miss R. Van Norman,
Mrs. Etta Van Nostrand, Dr. F.H. Van Nostrand, Mr. Lloyd
Watson, Mr. Donald A. Webster, Mr. J. Murray Wood.

CONTENTS

All around on the streets of Aurora are symbols of our past and present. There are parts of town where century-old buildings rub shoulders with modern bungalows, stores, or apartment buildings. There is a sense here of a community whose roots lie deep in the past, even as Aurora grows and prospers just a few kilometres away from Canada's largest city.

This book is for all those who have come to call Aurora home or who have come to love its streets, its buildings, and its people. It will tell a story which is already familiar to a few. But for many of its readers, it will provide a first glimpse of their community's past.

In these pages are many reasons for hope and encouragement; for here are many scenes which will be recognizable today, which prove that succeeding generations of Aurorans have cared about their community and tended it carefully. Other pages may tell a different story: they will show buildings and streetscapes which have gone forever and left us poorer without them.

This is not just a book about buildings and streets, however. It is also about people and how they went about their daily lives. Some of these people may be well known, but most are not. By seeing them at work and at play, perhaps we can see our own lives and our own times in broader perspective.

Our history is a fragile thing, too easily lost or forgotten. As I sorted through the photographs to be used in this book, I was reminded of a story told me by Donald Webster, who taught for many years at the old Aurora Public School on Church Street. Don was always interested in local history and told me one day a student of his had brought a few glass negatives to class to show him. The student had picked them up from a man who was scraping off their shadowy images in order to build a greenhouse. These negatives had once belonged to Robert Newbery, one of Aurora's first photographers. Don offered his students five cents a negative for any more they could salvage, but he was too late. Important records from our past had been destroyed by one man's thoughtless actions.

Another Auroran, Jesse M. Walton, began gathering local artifacts and documents in the 1930s, but there was no organized historical society until Aurora's centennial year in 1963, and no museum until a decade after that. In those early years, T. Howard Oliver did more than any other to ensure that early pictures which still remained in private hands would be copied and saved for posterity. Following his death, some of Howard's many friends contributed to a memorial fund which helped the Aurora and District Historical Society continue the work he had pioneered.

Once the Aurora Museum had been established through a co-operative agreement between the historical society and the Town of Aurora, the tasks of researching, storing, preserving, and displaying became a little easier. At first, all work at the museum, which from 1973 to 1981 was located in the old Aurora waterworks building on Yonge Street, was accomplished by volunteers and summer student employees. Since 1981 — thanks to the Society, the Town, and the Province of Ontario — the Aurora Museum has been housed in the Church Street School and has been able to employ Jacqueline Stuart as its curator. My thanks go to Jacqueline for the research which has allowed me to put dates on buildings or photographs which otherwise would have been much less precisely identified.

Also vital to the publication of this book has been the work of the Town of Aurora Heritage Committee under the guidance of Dr. G. Leslie Oliver. Among other functions, this committee recommends to Council properties which could be candidates for designation under the Ontario Heritage Act. In the course of its work, it must gather together a great deal of historical information for its files. I have freely drawn on those files in preparing this book and should acknowledge especially the work of Heritage Committee researcher Kathryn Anderson.

Other debts should be noted as well: one to Dr. James Johnston's book, *Aurora: Its Early Beginnings*, first published in 1963; another to the work of Jean Baker Pearce, particularly her series of articles in the *Aurora Banner* in 1967.

Dorothy Clark McClure has been an inspiration as well. Her sketches have led many to stop and think about Aurora's heritage for the first time.

In 1988, Aurora's 125th anniversary of incorporation, Aurora stands at a crossroads in time. Just as the coming of the railway in 1853 ushered in a whole new era of growth, so too will the current boom in residential, commercial, and industrial development mean irresistible change for Aurora. Aurora's official plan foresees a community where old and new will continue to play a part, where old buildings may find new uses, and where the historic core will be enhanced and invigorated. Whether Aurorans will have the desire and the opportunity to live up to these ideals is another matter. Only time will tell. This book will have done its part if it helps nourish interest in Aurora's past and enriches our future accordingly.

W. John McIntyre

Horton Place,
Aurora, Ontario, Canada,
February 1988.

Yonge Street, looking north from "Hutchinson's Hill," 1888

Yonge Street — named after British Secretary of War Sir George Yonge and started by order of Lieutenant-Governor John Graves Simcoe in 1794 as a route between York (Toronto) and Holland Landing — opened the townships of King and Whitchurch to settlement. By 1806, all the land on both sides of the road within present-day Aurora had been claimed. In 1888, when this picture was taken from a point near today's Henderson Drive, the area already was known as an old and well-established farming community. That same year, just to the north, the village of Aurora officially became a town.

Wellington Street, looking east from Victoria Street, c.1910

Wellington Street — named after the Duke of Wellington, who defeated Napoleon at the Battle of Waterloo — gave access to the forests and farmlands of Whitchurch township to the east and King township to the west. Farmers used the road to bring grain and lumber to the mills powered by the creeks which flowed through the village. Their business at the mill complete, they might then stop to trade at the stores at the crossroads of Wellington and Yonge.

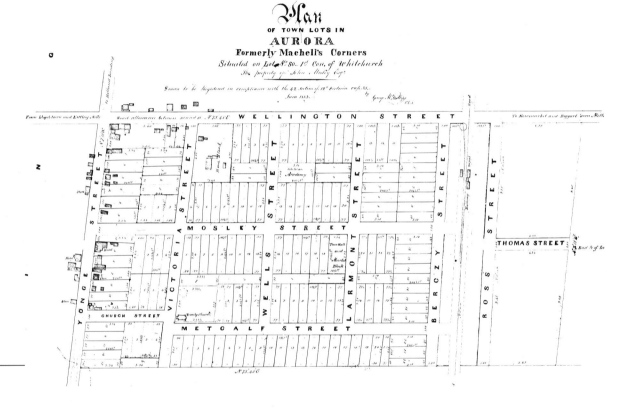

Plan of Aurora, 1854

It was the arrival of Ontario's first railway — the Ontario, Simcoe & Huron — in 1853 that inspired John Mosley to subdivide his farm into building lots. Before the railway came, the village had been known as Machell's Corners, while its post office went by the name "Whitchurch." The railway, however, heralded the dawn of a new era and prompted postmaster Charles Doan to propose a new name for the community, "Aurora," after the Greek goddess of the dawn. Mosley knew that new factories and businesses would be eager to locate close to the railway line and that their employees would need places to live.

Mosley's plan shows that some careful attention already had gone into village planning. Church Street was aligned in such a way that it provided a vista from Yonge Street east to Trinity Church. While the proposed academy shown on Wells Street was never constructed, in 1867 the village council bought the entire block of land bounded by Wells, Metcalfe, Larmont, and Mosley streets for a park.

Looking toward Aurora from the northwest, c.1890

On a lazy summer afternoon a hundred years ago, this was the view down into the valley of Aurora, from a field on Bathurst Street, north of Wellington. In this photograph large stumps still mark the spot where virgin timber once flourished, while snake fences mark off farmers' fields. In the twentieth century, much of this land returned to forest and bush, only to be cleared again — this time for streets and houses.

Plan of Match-Ville (Aurora) 1853

Probably unhappy about the prospect of a new name, "Aurora," for Machell's Corners, Richard Machell subdivided his land just north of Wellington Street and called it "Match-Ville." Needless to say, "Aurora" was more popular.

It has been suggested that the name "Match-Ville" was chosen because of the presence of an early match factory. A more likely explanation is that "Match-Ville" sounded a lot like "Machell." In fact, even the surveyor was confused, spelling Machell's name "Matchell." Perhaps "Match-Ville" was supposed to have been "Mach-Ville"?

Map of Aurora from Miles and Company's "Illustrated Historical Atlas of the County of York", 1878

The creeks and mill pond which supported Aurora's early industrial growth, along with the railway line which brought new prosperity in the 1850s, are clearly visible here. Also marked are the sites of Baldwin's flour mill, a potash works, a planing mill, a tannery, a carriage factory, and a "rope walk," a long narrow building where rope was made. Wilkinson's implement factory and the Fleury foundry are also shown. Important village institutions such as the post office, schoolhouse, bank, two hotels, Temperance Hall, Masonic Hall, Mechanics' Hall (incorrectly located), the Town Hall and Market, the Drill Hall, and the railway station also appear here, as do Trinity Anglican Church and no less than three Methodist churches — Wesleyan Methodist, Primitive Methodist, and Methodist Episcopal.

At the southern edge of the village is the "Aurora Driving Park," used for fairs and horse racing. Across Kennedy Street are "Park Lots," oversized lots which were intended for large houses and gardens. Just to the north is Lepper Street, named after Matthew Lepper, an early merchant and village reeve. Years later, residents of the street decided poor Matthew Lepper's name sounded too much like a disease and successfully petitioned to have the name changed to "Hillview Road."

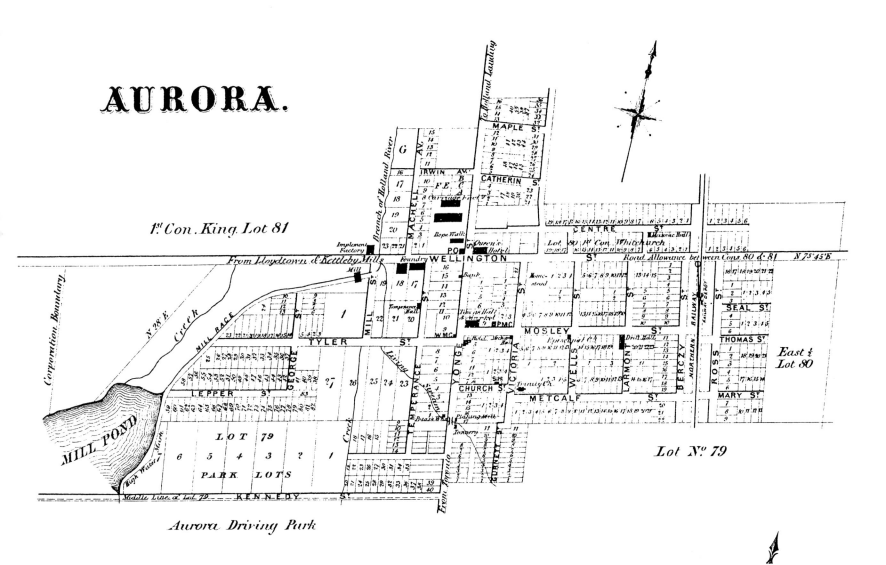

AURORA.

Aurora Driving Park

Yonge Street, looking north from Tyler Street, c.1870

These village buildings were almost exclusively of frame construction, and only three have survived the several fires and waves of rebuilding which have swept along this part of Yonge Street. Like most commercial buildings of the time, they look much like houses, appropriate to an era when most shopowners lived upstairs from, or at the back of, their places of business. While no traffic is visible to prevent pedestrians from crossing Yonge Street, the mud must have presented its own special hazards.

Yonge Street, looking south from the Methodist (United) Church tower at Tyler Street, c.1890

A mixture of houses and shops characterized this section of Yonge Street from Tyler Street south past Church Street. Several of these buildings survive today, in varying states of preservation.

"Log Cabin at Aurora," from a postcard, c.1908

This log house, which stood at the south end of Aurora on Ridge Road West, was built out of logs using methods brought to Canada by American settlers. Surveyor Augustus Jones reported that at least six such houses had been erected within the present town limits by June 1798.

Today two early log houses remain on their original sites within the boundaries of Aurora. The best preserved is the Jonathan Petch house, built on Leslie Street, just north of Wellington. Another is contained within the former Jack Woods farmhouse at the east corner of Edward Street and Allaura Boulevard.

"Castle Doan" (built early 1800s),
Yonge Street

This saltbox-shaped house at the north corner of Yonge Street and Catherine Avenue was built of timber frame construction, using finely hewn timbers held together by pegged mortice-and-tenon joints. Its date of construction is unknown. By the 1840s, it was the home of Charles and Catherine Doan and served as the village's first post office.

It is hard to imagine that this house was demolished in a few hours on July 2, 1982. Preservationists had been lulled into a false sense of security by reports that private investors were planning to move the house and repair it. Only its six-panelled front door, some early twelve-over-twelve window sash, and some pieces of baseboard and chair rail from the interior were saved. They now form part of a room setting at the Aurora Museum.

"Doan Hall" (built 1855), Yonge Street

Shown here in the 1950s, *Doan Hall* was one of Aurora's first brick houses. Its balanced façade suggested the lingering influence of Georgian design, while its Gothic-arched sidelights by the front door and its large Italianate brackets at the eaves heralded the beginning of interest in other, more exotic styles of architecture. Charles Doan built this house in 1855 on the west side of Yonge Street, just north of Wellington. It stood as a symbol of faith in the new community whose growth was assured by the arrival of the railway and which Doan had renamed "Aurora."

As with the much earlier *Castle Doan*, it is inconceivable that in 1969 this house was demolished. Demolition came in spite of an imaginative scheme put forward by citizens prior to Aurora's centennial year in 1963, suggesting that *Doan Hall* be used as reading rooms for an expanded Aurora Public Library which could have been erected behind. Instead, the library was located on Victoria Street and *Doan Hall* made way for Doane Hall Pharmacy.

Gower house (built 1856), Berczy Street

On 4 July 1856, this house was offered for sale in the New-market *New Era* newspaper:

> A comfortable two story dwelling house, newly erected, with every suitable convenience for the residence of a genteel family . . . situated opposite the railway station. The premises are in excellent order and well fenced. There is also a well of excellent water. The location is healthy and desirable, being within one hour's ride of Toronto by railway.

It is a good example of Georgian design at its simplest, balanced and well proportioned. Here members of the Gower and Irwin families are shown in front of the house in this turn-of-the-century photograph.

The house survives today, drastically altered.

Henry Machell house (built c.1861),
Wellington Street East

This recent photograph shows what is probably Aurora's most important surviving house from its early days as a village. It was owned by the Machell family whose general store was less than half a block away at the southeast corner of Yonge and Wellington streets and who gave the name "Machell's Corners" to the village itself.

Despite its busy location, this house has been well maintained as a residence. It features a centre door with rectangular transom and sidelights framed by Doric pilasters and a simple entablature. While its clapboard siding has been covered with stucco, it retains its original windows, old louvered shutters, decorative corner boards, and returned eaves.

John Field house (built 1861-62),
Wellington Street East

Like the Henry Machell house, this frame house was clad in stucco many years after it was built, but still retains its balanced Georgian proportions. The upstairs window sashes shown in this photograph from the 1960s also were changed. The windows below once were in the form of French doors opening onto a broad verandah. That verandah was removed and the present front porch, modelled after one near Manchester, Massachusetts, was added about 1920.

The first owner of this house was John Field, a business partner and adopted son of Richard Machell. In 1878, it was purchased by Dr. John Rutherford, Aurora's first mayor. Rutherford's son-in-law, Dr. Chester Richardson, lived and practised here from 1903 until 1910. From 1910 to 1974 it was the home and office of Dr. Garnet W. Williams. Today it continues its long-standing association with the medical profession as the Aurora Family Health Clinic.

"The Tailor's House" (built c.1862), *Wellington Street East*

Edward and Mary Andrews purchased this property late in 1861 and lived in this house with their eleven children. Edward Andrews kept a tailoring shop next door. The house remained in the ownership of an Andrews descendant until 1978. Today it serves as The Tailor's House Restaurant. Its similar neighbour to the east also has found a commercial use.

Trinity Anglican Rectory (built 1862), Metcalfe Street, from a photograph taken 1895

While its front verandah and balcony were remodelled in 1918, Trinity Anglican rectory still stands today on spacious grounds behind Trinity Church. Here, the Rev. Horace Mussen and his family are enjoying a pleasant afternoon in the summer of 1895.

House on Centre Street (built 1860s)

A good example of a style and shape very popular in Ontario, this house has a steep Gothic gable at the centre of its façade. This one-and-a-half-storey plan gave nearly as much living space as a full two-storey house, although it was taxed at a lower rate.

On the back of this photograph, taken from a postcard dated October 1919, is the message,

> here is where we live
> walk in and have a piece
> of pie
> Aunt E

*Dr. Hillary's house on Wellington Street East,
from a photograph c.1870*

In the foreground of this picture stands the home of Dr. Robert W. Hillary and his family prior to their move to *The Manor* on Yonge Street. Even here Dr. Hillary's fondness for the Gothic style may be seen in this house's steeply pitched gables, king posts, and bargeboard ("gingerbread"). The Hillarys moved here in 1861. This house survived in greatly altered condition until 1968, when it made way for the present Aurora Post Office.

Hillary House (built 1862), Yonge Street

Traditionally known as *The Manor*, this house has been home to members of the Hillary family since 1876. It was built in 1862 by Dr. Walter B. Geikie, a prominent Toronto physician and teacher. In 1869, Dr. Geikie sold it to Dr. Frederick W. Strange who added an elaborate billiard room at the back. Dr. Strange, in turn, sold the house to Dr. Robert William Hillary, who is shown here with members of his family around 1880. Among Dr. Hillary's improvements were a new kitchen wing and what may have been Aurora's first indoor bathroom.

The house is an excellent example of the Gothic Revival style with elaborate bargeboard, a large verandah with bell-cast eaves, Gothic columns, and pointed arches. Its two front rooms were used as an examining room and a dispensary, while the rooms behind were for family use.

Hillary House is now owned by the Aurora and District Historical Society and plaqued by the National Historic Sites and Monuments Board of Canada. It too could have fallen victim to the bulldozer had it not been for the foresight and generosity of the Hillary family, the Historical Society, the Ontario Heritage Foundation, Parks Canada, several foundations, and corporate and individual donors. In the future it will be opened to the public as a museum.

This photograph, taken by Robert Newbery and found in the collection of the Markham District Historical Museum, provided the necessary documentation for the Historical Society's reconstruction of the original Gothic balcony railing, the only major exterior element of Hillary House which had not survived until modern times.

Hillary House (built 1862), Yonge Street

The south lawn and wide verandah of Hillary House provided a welcome retreat on a summer day near the turn of the century. Shown here are a small conservatory and sunroom, not original to the house and removed many years ago.

"Horton Place" (built 1875), Yonge Street

Horton Place boldly proclaimed the popularity of the Italianate style with its round-headed windows and doors, ornamental brackets, bay windows, and cast iron cresting. It was built for Dr. Alfred Robinson and his family who are seen spilling out of doors and onto balconies in this photograph taken about 1880. Dr. Robinson, a dental surgeon, named his house Horton Place after his family's former home in Bradford, Yorkshire. As the family grew, the Robinson girls offered French lessons in a room upstairs and taught dancing in the big rooms below. From another room came the sounds of Dr. Robinson's drill, declared to be painless through the use of nitrous oxide gas. In the barn at the back of the house Dr. Robinson kept his horse and carriage for his regular office hours in faraway places such as Mount Albert, Bradford, Stouffville, Markham, Richmond Hill, and Nobleton.

"Horton Place" (built 1875), Yonge Street

Charles Webster and his wife, Della Petch Webster, posed in front of *Horton Place* soon after buying the house from the Robinsons in 1901. It is owned by Webster descendants today. As a girl, Della Petch dreamed of living in the big house on the hill. Her dream came true in 1901, and with it the installation of hot water radiators, electricity, hardwood floors, indoor plumbing, and other amenities of turn-of-the-century living.

Mrs. Webster was a tireless political worker and opened *Horton Place* and its spacious grounds to innumerable social and political gatherings. Charles Webster worked as manager of the Fleury works.

*Inglehurst (built 1876),
Yonge Street*

Inglehurst, with Hillary House and *Horton Place*, was one of the three grand Victorian houses which stood at the northern entrance to Aurora and gave the area the nickname "Nob Hill." Its asymmetrical façade with Gothic Revival detail reflected the late Victorian trend to break free from the restraints of Georgian balance entirely.

Recent research indicates that *Inglehurst* was designed for foundry owner Joseph Fleury in 1876 by the Toronto firm of Langley, Langley and Burke. Fleury enjoyed his new house for only four years, however. He died in 1880 while serving as both reeve of the village and warden of the County of York. His son, Herbert W. Fleury, took over the house and lived there until his death in 1940, spending long periods of time alone while his wife and daughter lived in France.

Like other large houses of Aurora, *Inglehurst* was built on the village's busy main street and was a focal point for community, as well as family, pride. It too hosted many public functions, serving for instance as the elegant venue for fund-raising Red Cross teas during the First World War.

In 1946, *Inglehurst* and many of its furnishings were acquired for Our Lady of Grace Church. The house was demolished in 1980 to make way for a church parking lot. Its massive front doors, a marble mantlepiece from the parlour, and other memorabilia were donated by the church to the Aurora Museum.

"The Carpenter's House" (built 1872), Wellington Street East

"The Carpenter's House" takes its name from its elaborate wooden trim and the fact that it was built by carpenter William Atkinson, who was responsible for building other frame houses in town as well. This is by far his most ambitious work, and shows the influence of the fanciful frame houses of the San Francisco Bay area of California, where Atkinson visited and eventually settled permanently.

Surprisingly, this elegant townhouse appears to have been built on speculation. Atkinson sold it to Annie Fry Hillary, wife of Dr. Robert William Hillary, who rented it to tenants.

In recent years the house gained attention in the pages of John I. Rempel's book, *Building with Wood*. Since this photograph was taken in 1977, the house has undergone extensive restoration.

Roselawn (built 1870s), Maple Street

With its mansard roof, *Roselawn* represents what is often called the Second Empire style. Mansard-roofed buildings gained great popularity in France during the reign of Emperor Louis Napoleon. *Roselawn* may have been built by William Atkinson, builder of "The Carpenter's House." Certainly its combination of brackets, quoins, and bevelled siding is very similar. Most of this original detail now lies hidden under aluminum siding.

Reynolds House (built 1870s), Tyler Street

Again the combination of wooden quoins and bevelled siding suggests the work of William Atkinson; however, these details, along with brackets, doors, and window sash, were mass produced by this time. A carpenter had only to go to an establishment such as the nearby planing mill on Yonge Street to order as much machine-made ornament as his clients were willing to buy. Even so, these early details possessed a great deal more interest, variety, and charm than the aluminum or vinyl siding which now often hides them from view.

This house has an L-shaped plan which became very popular in Ontario towns during the last third of the nineteenth century. In front are Mrs. Robert Reynolds and her daughter.

Morrison-Walton House (built 1886) and Wellington Street East

Taken in the late 1920s, this photograph shows how Wellington Street, like Yonge, provided an elegant approach to Aurora. In the foreground on the right stands the Morrison-Walton house built by carriage-maker G.W. Morrison in 1886 and the home of Aurora businessman, mayor, and historian Jesse M. Walton from 1919 to 1945.

Whimster House (built 1892), Victoria Street

James Whimster, Aurora's own merchant prince, built this lofty house in High Victorian style. This was a time when stained and leaded glass was all the rage; darkly rich colours were in vogue; and gables, chimneys, and balconies were liable to turn up almost anywhere.

Whimster was the owner of a successful department store at the southeast corner of Wellington and Yonge streets, only a block away from this house. The store boasted two floors of merchandise and a broad stairway leading from one floor to the other. Despite his success, however, Whimster was known as a man who was careful with his money, exhorting his employees to save string and never sit down on the job.

Poplar Villa or The Château (built 1912), Yonge Street

This house originally was called *Poplar Villa*, but is better known to many as *The Château*, the name used when it operated as a tourist home that was particularly popular among newlywed couples. Its rounded corner tower with cone-shaped roof is reminiscent of a French château; however, there are elements of English Tudor added as well, making this a very typical Edwardian mix of styles.

The widening of Yonge Street in 1968-69 was particularly unkind to this fine house, effectively hiding it from most passersby and replacing its stone retaining wall with bare concrete capped by a pipe railing.

This photograph probably dates from the 1920s.

Wellington Street East from Victoria Street, late 1920s

The red brick houses in the foreground of this picture are typical of many built in Ontario towns during the first three decades of the twentieth century. They are solid and substantial and represent a turning away from Victorian ornamentation toward a more functional approach to architecture. Often their only decorative features are the stout columns and railings around their front verandahs, a leaded glass window or two, and solid oak woodwork inside.

The name of Aurora builder James Knowles is linked to many of these sturdy houses which may be found not only on Wellington Street, but on Catherine Avenue, Fleury Street, Wells Street, Kennedy Street West, and here and there in other parts of town as well.

Aurora Public School (built 1886), Church Street,
from a postcard c.1910

Designed by architect Thomas Kennedy and completed in 1886, the Aurora Public School combined elaborately patterned brickwork, a picturesque silhouette, and a belfry inspired by the architecture of British India. This building stood as a symbol of village pride and its faith in the power of education. It replaced an earlier school on the same site. In 1901, young Lester Bowles Pearson started school in the present Church Street building and there earned the local nickname "Smarty Pants Pearson" for his proficiency in Roman numerals.

In 1981, the Aurora Public School was plaqued by the Province of Ontario as a building of outstanding architectural significance. That year it became the home of the Aurora Museum and a recreational and cultural centre for the town. Only a few years earlier, however, some municipal politicians had called it an eyesore and fought to have it torn down to make way for a parking lot.

Aurora Public School Pupils, 1889

Spread across the front lawn and down the steps of the Aurora Public School is this substantial group of Aurora children believed to have been photographed in 1889, just three years after the school was built.

Aurora Public School Classroom,
January 1921

This room probably had changed little between the time the Aurora Public School was built in 1886 and the time this class was photographed in 1921. One important change, however, had been the installation in 1888 of the folding doors shown here on the right. These divided what once had been an open assembly room on the second floor into two rooms for the use of Aurora's first high school classes. The fixed rows of seats, the dark wainscot, the blackboards, and the clock all suggest an ideal of discipline and order.

This was Senior III, Miss Mabel Chappell's class.

HIGH SCHOOL AURORA ONT.

First Aurora High School (built 1892), Wells Street

Before this building was erected, the few Aurora young people who went on to further their education had to travel to Newmarket or, by the late 1880s, attend high-school-level classes in the Aurora Public School on Church Street. This sombre Romanesque building designed by Robert Ogilvie was built in 1892. Parts of it are said to have been incorporated into Aurora's second high school building, built in 1923 on the same site.

Aurora High School Girls' Basketball Team, 1911

These proper young ladies were members of their school basketball team during an era which expected modesty and decorum at all times.

From left to right they are:

Front row: Hattie Morgan, May Underhill, Marguerite Staples, Grace Brodie, and Lois Bond.

Back row: Elvira Manning, Bernice Charles, Mr. White (teacher), Ruby Bruce, Miss Van Duzer (teacher), Lena McCloskey, and Letoile Tustin.

Second Aurora High School (built 1923), Wells Street

This building replaced the first Aurora High School in 1923. Like its predecessor, it looked out onto the Town Park. Its larger size, however, suggests the greater importance given to secondary education by the 1920s. In style too it is different, providing an excellent example of the 1920s' return to the classical Georgian style. Since 1952, when the Aurora and District High School, later named The Dr. G.W. Williams Secondary School, opened on Dunning Avenue, this building has served as the Wells Street Public School.

School bus stuck in the snow, 1935

Getting to school from King township on a snowy day could pose all sorts of problems. Here (from left to right) Bob Walker, Jean Ross, Margaret Walker, and Ken Davis look on while Frank Egan and Bob Cain dig out.

Aurora High School Cadets on Victoria Street, 1940s

Cadet corps training was a part of life for Aurora high school students from the 1930s up until the 1960s.

Aurora High School Glee Club, 1948

Other memorable activities for several generations of Aurora students were music lessons from Illtyd Harris, shown here with his award-winning glee club on the front steps of the High School on Wells Street in 1948. The rule was white shirts and dark ties for the boys, white blouses and navy blue tunics for the girls. In rehearsal and in performance, Mr. Harris made choirs relax with his comic faces and gestures.

Mr. Harris stands on the top step at the far right. Principal J.H. Knowles stands at the far left.

De La Salle College (built 1916)

The Roman Catholic boys' school, De La Salle College, came to Aurora from downtown Toronto in 1916 and built this imposing building on "The Pinnacle" near the northwest corner of Yonge Street and Bloomington Road. De La Salle moved back to Toronto in 1949. Since then this building has served as a home for the developmentally handicapped and now is being renovated for use by several provincial government ministries.

Aurora   Ontario

Chapel

St. Andrews College

St. Andrews College

St. Andrew's College

St. Andrew's College moved to Aurora from Rosedale in Toronto in 1926. Architects for the original complex of buildings were the firm of Marani and Paisley who won an Ontario Society of Architects Medal for their design.

Today, St. Andrew's College continues to play an important role in the community and is one of Canada's foremost independent schools.

Aurora Flouring Mills, Wellington Street West, c.1900

While this picture dates only from the turn of the century, a mill was located on this site as early as 1845, run first probably by Jacob Hollingshead, then by the Irwin family, and finally by the Baldwin family, whose "Aurora Belle" flour was advertised as "Canada's Finest Pastry Flour."

The creeks running through Aurora provided an early source of power. One of them, Red Willow Creek, was dammed northwest of present-day Hillview Road. A mill race was built to control the flow of water from the pond to the mill located on the west corner of Mill Street and Wellington Street West.

As in many communities, a mill was probably Aurora's first industry. Once a mill was built, a cooper's shop was needed to supply barrels. To meet other needs of the farmers who brought their grain to the mill, a blacksmith's shop, a harness-maker's shop, and a general store followed.

The mill pictured here remained in operation until it was destroyed by fire in 1920. The Baldwins then relocated their business in a large brick building which still stands on the north side of Wellington Street East, beside the railway tracks.

Tannery workers (c.1890), Yonge Street

Tannery Creek provided fresh water for this early industry located on the east side of Yonge, just south of Church Street. It was begun by John T. Gurnett in 1858. Later it was owned by Edward Pease, who in 1879 built the large L-shaped buff brick house which still stands on the hill south of the tannery site. From 1878 until it closed, around 1905, the tannery was run by F.T. Daville.

Across the creek to the north was a planing mill which made wood siding, doors, windows, and shutters. On the opposite side of Yonge Street was a potash works which extracted lye from hardwood ashes in order to make soap. Earlier, a brewery had also been part of this pioneer industrial area.

*Atkinson House and blacksmith shop
(c.1900), Yonge Street*

Not far from the tannery, on the opposite side of the street, stood Arthur Atkinson's house and blacksmith shop and a small carriage factory. The mansard-roofed house to the north belonged to Arthur's parents, Joseph and Mary Atkinson.

Like many other early craftsmen, businessmen, and entrepreneurs, Atkinson lived next door to his work. Houses coexisted comfortably alongside small workshops and stores during a time before zoning by-laws created separate residential, commercial, and industrial areas.

*H.J. Charles Carriage and Waggon Works
(c.1880), Yonge Street*

The H.J. Charles Carriage and Waggon Works was located on the northwest corner of Yonge Street and St. John's Sideroad until 1887. The carriages and wagons proudly displayed out front recall a time when even the need for transportation vehicles could be met by village craftsmen.

Weigh scale (1914), Berczy Street

The coming of the railway in 1853 meant that village products, along with livestock and produce from neighbouring farms, now could easily be sent to market in Toronto. This weigh scale, located on the west side of the tracks, was used to help calculate the appropriate charges for shipment.

From left to right are Mr. Coulter, Walter Yule, Benjamin F. Davis, and H.W. Wright, while Bill Sodden is sitting in the sleigh inside the building.

Creamery (c.1905-1910), Yonge Street

William Osborne is shown here inside Charles Campbell's creamery in the gable-fronted brick building which still stands halfway between Centre Street and Catherine Avenue.

Creameries were first established in Ontario in the 1870s. Buying cream from local farmers, these establishments churned it into butter for sale in stores. This marked the end of an era when virtually every household had made its own butter.

The Fleury works (c.1910), Wellington Street West

At the turn of the century, J. Fleury's Sons was by far Aurora's largest employer, turning out ploughs and a wide variety of other agricultural implements for shipment throughout Canada. The business was started by Joseph Fleury, a blacksmith, in 1859. He had moved here from King township in order to take advantage of Aurora's favourable location on the railway line. Fleury's business prospered and diversified, even briefly including the manufacture of sewing machines in the 1870s.

Joseph died in 1880, leaving the business to his sons. Thereafter Herbert W. Fleury oversaw the operation. Hard hit by the depression of the 1930s and competition from larger firms such as Massey-Harris, J. Fleury's Sons amalgamated with the Bissell company of Elora in 1937 and ended operations here in 1941. Fleury-Bissell implements and parts continued on the market, however, until the late 1960s.

The buildings shown here stretch from the office on the east corner of Wellington and Temperance streets west to Mill Street. Many of them are used today as warehouses. Their proximity to Aurora's downtown core, their solid construction and architectural detail all suggest that these buildings may someday find another, more public use as offices, stores, or apartments. Certainly their demolition would be a great loss to the community.

Fleury workers, c.1900

These men represent the more than 200 workers J. Fleury's Sons employed at the height of its operation. In their spare time, when not casting parts for ploughs, they made decorative items such as cast iron ships and iron frogs for use as doorstops.

Fleury office, 15 October 1910

Shown here at work in the Fleury office are manager Charles Webster, his secretary, Miss Viola Petch, and an unidentified clerk. A few years earlier, Miss Petch's adventurous young sister, Eva, had climbed up the tall smokestack at the Fleury works and ceremoniously put the final brick in place. That smokestack stands as a landmark today, although it has not been used for nearly fifty years. The office itself, however, is gone. It stood on the east corner of Temperance Street and Wellington Street West.

Collis Leather Company (1913), Tyler Street

Collis Leather, established just one year before this picture was taken, was located on Tannery Creek downstream from Collis's predecessors on Yonge Street. The Collis house stands almost opposite the tannery, at the top of the hill.

T. Sisman shoe factory and residence, Berczy and Mosley streets, from a panoramic photograph c.1925

In 1901, the Underhill and Sisman Shoe Manufacturing Company moved to Aurora from Markham and built the brick factory shown toward the right of this panoramic photograph. In 1910, the Underhill-Sisman partnership was dissolved. Underhill stayed in the old factory for a short time, while the new T. Sisman Shoe Company built the large factory shown here on the left, at the south corner of Mosley and Berczy streets. Thomas Sisman and his family lived opposite the new factory in a house renowned for its beautiful gardens and grounds. Sisman's continued in operation until 1985. The house and most of the factory have been demolished; however, the 1901 Underhill and Sisman building survives today as offices.

Sisman shoe factory interior, showing workers and finished shoes, c.1920

Machines and work benches were lined up by the windows of the old factory at Mosley and Berczy streets to take advantage of natural light and ventilation. Still, factories like this posed many dangers if a worker grew careless or if one of the many overhead belts broke and flew loose.

Direct Importations. *Cash and Barter Store.*

Charles Doan's general store and post office, northwest corner of Yonge and Wellington streets, from an engraving in the "Aurora Banner", 26 February 1864

Invoice from D.W. Doan, 21 September 1878

Charles Doan, Aurora's first reeve and postmaster, opened this store in 1854. Shown in this newspaper advertisement are several ploys to catch the eye of potential customers: bolts of patterned cloth hanging from the upstairs windows, merchandise displayed on the wooden sidewalk outside, and a sign, "Cash for Wheat," to waylay farmers coming into town.

In earlier years, this site was the location of what was probably Aurora's first school, a one-room log building. Today, it is occupied by the Bank of Montreal.

By 1878, David W. Doan was running his father's business at Wellington and Yonge streets.

This printed form suggests the wide and varied array of goods available at his store. They included "homeopathic specifics" recalling a system of medical practice which believes that disease can be cured by minute doses of medicine which produce effects similar to a patient's symptoms. Doan's stock also included a supply of eyeglasses and "Hastings' Strictly Pure Wine."

Bank of Montreal (built 1922), northwest corner of Yonge and Wellington streets

Ontario Bank, northwest corner of Yonge and Wellington streets, c.1890

In 1888, David Doan's store had been remodelled for use by the Ontario Bank. Many of its original features remained, however. Its Georgian design, with brick quoins at the corners, had been intended to complement *Doan Hall* which stood just to the north.

On the corner is an oil-burning street lamp.

In 1922, the old Doan store was demolished. While Aurora lost an important landmark, it gained this handsome building with its classical entranceway and coat of arms above. Its main floor was for business; an apartment for the bank manager and his family was located upstairs. It was similar to many other bank buildings erected across Canada at the time. Its two-storey height complemented that of the earlier buildings around it and gave it a sense of dignity and importance at the heart of Aurora. It was demolished in 1973.

Yonge Street, south from Wellington Street,
from a postcard c.1910

On this summer day, Yonge Street was fairly quiet. Awnings were extended to protect both merchandise and passersby from the glare of the sun.

On both sides of the street hydro poles, electric wires, and telephone lines were much in evidence. The technology they symbolized must have seemed both wonderful and exciting, and definitely not something to be hidden away or buried under the sidewalks.

At about the middle of the block, on the east side, can be seen Aurora's Boer War memorial. In 1899-1900 seven Aurora men volunteered for service with the British forces in South Africa. Britain's success was commemorated by this cast-iron memorial which featured the practical combination of a lamp standard on top and a drinking fountain and horsetrough below. It was moved to the Town Park in 1933 and later destroyed.

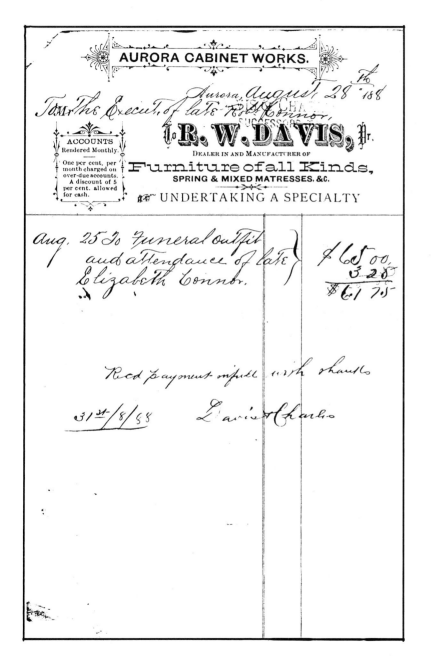

AURORA CABINET WORKS.

Aurora, August 28 th 188

To Mr The Execut. of late Ro. Connor,

R. W. DAVIS, Jr.

DEALER IN AND MANUFACTURER OF

Furniture of all Kinds,

SPRING & MIXED MATRESSES. &C.

UNDERTAKING A SPECIALTY

ACCOUNTS Rendered Monthly.
One per cent. per month charged on over-due accounts. A discount of 5 per cent. allowed for cash.

Aug. 25 To Funeral outfit and attendance of late Elizabeth Connor. $65 00,
3 25
$61 75

Recd payment in full with thanks

31st/8/88   Davis & Charles

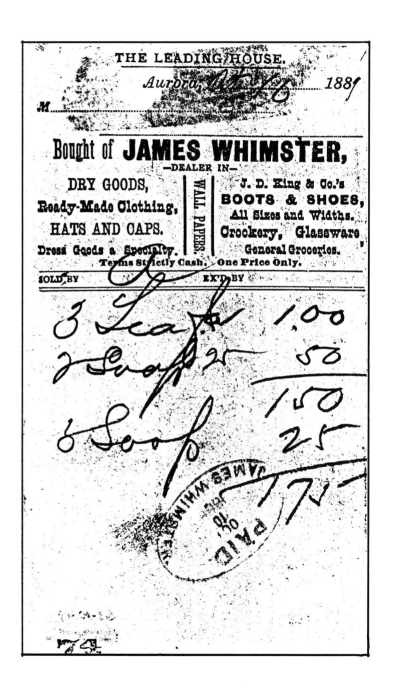

THE LEADING HOUSE.

Aurora, ... 188

M ....

Bought of JAMES WHIMSTER,

—DEALER IN—

DRY GOODS,

Ready-Made Clothing,

HATS AND CAPS.

Dress Goods a Specialty.

Terms Strictly Cash.

WALL PAPERS.

J. D. King & Co.'s
BOOTS & SHOES,
All Sizes and Widths.
Crockery, Glassware
General Groceries.
One Price Only.

SOLD BY   EX'D BY

3 Tea   1.00
2 Soap 25   50
1 50
1 Soap   25
1 75

PAID JAMES WHIMSTER

Bills from William Willis and Son saddlery (1887), the Aurora Cabinet Works (1888), and James Whimster, general merchants (1899)

These three bills display the Victorian printer's art and the decorative detail that was lavished on even the most humble printed form.

The Aurora Cabinet Works bill documents the close link which often existed between furniture-making and undertaking. The skills of a cabinetmaker were needed for coffins just as they were for tables or chests of drawers. In Aurora, this link continues today through the Thompson family's operation, since 1921, of both a retail furniture business and a funeral home.

James Whimster's invoice lists the wide variety of merchandise available at "The Leading House" in the building which still stands at the southeast corner of Yonge and Wellington streets. Like Timothy Eaton, Whimster advertised "Terms Strictly Cash" and "One Price Only." These were relatively new developments in the retail trade. In Charles and David Doan's time, farm produce, butter, eggs, and meat often were accepted in exchange for merchandise. Also, merchants and their customers often haggled over prices, the lowest price going to the best haggler.

Tokens from Towns and Company, general merchants, and R.J. Evans, baker, c.1900

Towns and Company, like other merchants of the time, offered their customers tokens instead of cash when they made change. Or they might give out tokens as premiums. In either case, they hoped to encourage customers to come back and shop there again.

Bakers such as R.J. Evans, in Aurora from about 1878 to 1894, probably sold their customers tokens on a regular basis. The tokens could be left at the door more safely than cash in exchange for a loaf of bread from Mr. Evans's delivery wagon.

Interior of Eade's Aurora Hardware, west side of Yonge Street, c.1910

One could hardly ask for a better view of the stock of a small-town hardware store from seventy-five years ago than that which is offered here. Eade's Aurora Hardware was located in the 1875 Faughner Block, which still stands half a block south of Wellington Street. From left to right are Mrs. Eade, Norm Eade, and "Mike" Stephens.

Ough's hardware, west side of Yonge Street, c.1915

Ough's hardware store offered a wide range of essential goods, including the latest in McClary stoves and furnaces. It was located north of Eade's, in a building partly destroyed by fire in 1954. Out front was a portent of things to come: a gas pump to fuel the new-fangled horseless carriage. On 5 May 1911, the *Aurora Banner* reported "Mr. Wm Ough, sr., has the honour of being the first person in the Town to purchase an automobile. It arrived here Thursday and Mr. Ough and family have enjoyed several trips with it."

"Aurora Banner" office, west side of Yonge
Street, c.1900

Here at the press are editor and publisher Sylvester Lundy;
his son, Charles; and Michael Carolan, linotype operator.

The *Aurora Banner*, Aurora's oldest continuing business,
started publication in 1864 and was closely associated with the
Lundy family during much of its early history. It was Aurora's
second newspaper. Its predecessor, the *Aurora Sun*, had lasted
for only a few months in 1858. During the 1880s, the tabloid-
style *Aurora Borealis* operated as a competitor to the *Banner*,
the *Banner* openly supporting the Liberal party while the *Borealis* adamantly campaigned for the Conservatives.

Towns and Norris grocery and dry goods store, west side of Yonge Street, 1919

The "Welcome Home" sign displayed here suggests that this picture was taken just after the First World War when Aurora boys were coming home.

From left to right are a travelling salesman just arrived by the Metropolitan Radial Railway, Pearl Borden, Lillian Smith, Mrs. Turp, and Mr. Gregory.

Medical Hall (built 1885) and Stevenson Block, east side of Yonge Street

Medical Hall is downtown Aurora's only "skyscraper." It was the tallest building there when when it was built in 1885 and remains the tallest building today, a local landmark which can be seen from as far away as Bathurst Street. It was built by druggist Henry J. Hartman, who took ill with consumption during its construction and died soon after it was finished. In 1886 it was purchased by Dr. John Rutherford and managed by Charles Willis. Willis's son, John F., took over the store about 1910. Charles's grandson, also John F. Willis, took over in 1955 and operated a pharmacy there until 1969.

The second floor once housed the *Aurora Banner* office, while the third floor was home to the Royal Templars of Temperance and, later, the Loyal Orange Lodge and the Aurora Town Band. Today the building's links with medicine continue through the dentists' offices located on the second floor.

Architecturally, this building is distinguished by an oriel window, patterned brickwork, and an elaborate brick cornice.

The wooden Stevenson Block to the south looks like something from a western boomtown. It was replaced by the present two-storey brick buildings on the site about 1910.

Interior of F.E. York drug store, west side of Yonge Street, c.1910

Although smaller than Medical Hall, York's drug store also carried a wide variety of patent medicines, toiletries, fancy goods, and candy, as well as filling prescriptions.

While both families were in the same business, the Willises and the Yorks were related by marriage, and that must have put a damper on too much competition.

Anthony Caruso in front of his store, west side of Yonge Street, 1930s

The Caruso family's fruit and vegetable market has been located here since 1913, making it the oldest continuing retail business in Aurora. Here Tony Caruso stands in front of his store amidst an abundance of fresh fruit and vegetables.

Morris butcher shop, south side of Wellington Street East, c.1920

Wellington Street, just east of Yonge, has long been home to Aurora butcher shops. The Morris butcher shop shown here was demolished in 1964 to make way for the expansion of First Baptist Church. Just to the west, however, one butcher shop remains in operation today, just as it has since 1885. From 1885 until 1976, it was run by the Knowles family.

Shown here in the doorway of the Morris shop is Russell Heaney. On the sidewalk stands Fred Morris, while "Old Dog Trail" looks on, probably hoping for a bone.

The Lloyd Building (built 1882), southwest corner of Yonge and Wellington streets

John Lloyd, a bookseller and stationer, built this building with its ornate metal cornice in 1882. Two years later, Lloyd opened Aurora's first telephone exchange here. In 1903, an addition was made to the west end when the building became home to a general store operated by Thomas Caster and Allen Davey. From 1913 to 1917, the Lloyd building was home to the Imperial Bank of Canada, shown in this photographic postcard. Since then this building has housed a wide variety of retail outlets, including a branch of Dominion Stores. It stands today much as it has for over a century, providing a strong link with the past at Aurora's main downtown corner.

Interior of J.M. Walton bank, west side of Yonge Street, 1905

Gleaming wood counters and polished brass wickets added a sense of solidity, quality, and tradition to turn-of-the-century bank interiors such as this one. A lighter touch was provided by an elaborate wallpaper border and a papered ceiling on which electrical wires recently had been strung.

J.M. Walton operated his banking business here before he moved to more spacious quarters on the other side of Yonge Street. This photograph shows the north end of the 1875 Faughner Block, which still stands today. In the cellar below, the old bank vault is still in place.

J.M. Walton bank, east side of Yonge Street, c.1910

In 1909 Jesse Walton moved his bank to the east side of Yonge Street to a building which stands today, among the oldest downtown. It started out as a small frame building with its gable end facing the street. Around the turn of the century, it was modernized by means of a high false front to make it look as if were a full two storeys high. This false front was made of brick and has a decorative cornice and a projecting oriel window. Today the huge safe from banking days remains in place, although in recent years this building has been home to McConnell's jewellery store.

Aurora Post Office (built 1914-15), east side of Yonge Street

This impressive Italianate-style building combined Aurora's post office, custom house, and town clock when it was built in 1914-15. In many ways, it became Aurora's most important meeting place. Before home delivery, everyone came to the post office at least once a day to pick up mail in a spacious lobby trimmed with marble, brass, and polished oak. Townsfolk set their watches by the post office's lighted clock. Since the building was set back from the street, it provided a logical site for outdoor meetings, and bands played there for street dances.

In 1968, the post office moved to Wellington Street. Its new owner has carefully maintained the building's façade, however, and continues to keep the clock lighted and in good working order.

Aurora Dairy (built 1938), Yonge and Centre streets

The Aurora Dairy building was typical of 1930s architecture. It recalled that decade's reaction against Victorian ornamentation. While Aurora's late nineteenth century commercial buildings were enlivened by brick and metal cornices, finials, and other decorative details, the 1930s demanded a more functional approach. That approach is evident here, relieved only by clipped-corner windows and some Art Deco striping on its glass-tiled façade.

In its heyday, this was a thriving local business and a popular gathering spot after a movie at the old Royal Theatre just a few yards to the east, on the south side of Centre Street.

The Aurora Dairy building was demolished in 1984.

Bell Telephone exchange and Cousins Dairy, Yonge and Mosley streets, late 1930s

By the 1920s, Aurora had enough telephone subscribers to warrant the construction of this brick and stone building on the south corner of Yonge and Mosley streets.

Just to the south was Cousins Dairy in a "streamlined" building from the 1930s.

Interior of Bell Telephone exchange, Yonge Street, 1940s

"Number, please" were the familiar words of any one of these operators. From left to right they are: Ellamae Blake Carson, Marie Hulme, Ruth Rothwell, Doris Payne, Claire Fortier, Ruth Rose, and Jean Giles.

Scanlon Bakery vehicles and drivers,
late 1930s

The Scanlon Bakery was located on the east side of Yonge Street, just south of the old post office. It was housed in an 1850s frame building which in 1926 was clad in brick. Its elegant display windows with brass trim and leaded-glass transoms are still there, as are a classical archway and fanlight which once separated the bakery sales area from a china shop. At the back are leaded-glass casement windows which look out onto a tiny walled garden.

Richard Scanlon opened his bakery in 1886. His son-in-law, Charles Peterson, expanded the business. By 1939, Scanlon's had eight branch stores. Cottagers stopped at Scanlon's in Aurora on their way north on Yonge Street: anyone who knew Aurora at all knew Scanlon's and its fine breads, cakes, pies, tarts, and pastries. The delivery fleet shown here, including a horse-drawn wagon for local deliveries, was needed to keep all of Scanlon's branches and their customers supplied.

In 1970, the Scanlon name disappeared, the bakery's new owners deciding to make only butter tarts, which are produced at a different site in town and are marketed as "Granny's Tarts." In recent years, the building itself has been neglected and now awaits some imaginative new owner to bring it to life once more.

Yonge Street South from Wellington Street,
c.1940

While businesses have come and gone, most of the buildings shown in this picture remain today — one significant exception being Aurora's 1875 Town Hall. Its tower is visible here in the distance, near the north corner of Yonge and Mosley streets. It once completed the vista punctuated by the "skyscraper" Medical Hall and the post office clock tower.

When this picture was taken, downtown was Aurora's only shopping centre. Now plazas to the north, south, east, and west have drained business away and heavy traffic has made parking difficult. Recent efforts to revive downtown shopping often have met with apathy or downright opposition. Lack of commercial growth downtown may have had one good effect, however: it has eased the pressure for demolition and rebuilding and left many fine nineteenth and early twentieth century buildings intact. Now that developers are becoming more aware of the merits of recycling older buildings and shoppers are becoming bored with strip plazas, perhaps Aurora's historic core will come back to life again.

Children with their toys, c.1900

These four cousins posed with their toys in Robert Newbery's Aurora studio around the turn of the century. Behind them is one of Newbery's standard backdrops, a painted scene suggesting a grand entrance hall complete with a staircase and potted palms. The backdrop ends rather abruptly at the left, where the camera caught the panel's edge.

From left to right are Fred Powell, Elma Powell, Grace Petch, and Gladys Petch, posed with their cat and dog. What a task it must have been to pose these children, arrange their toys, and keep the cat and dog still long enough for the picture to be taken. In 1888, Newbery had advertised in *The Aurora Borealis*,

"Babies Taken on the Jump." Evidently he had a way with children!

Their toys helped teach these children important lessons: the bank taught the importance of saving and thrift, while the stove, carpet sweeper, dolls, doll carriage, bed, dresser, and tea set introduced young girls to the task of running a house and raising children. Many turn-of-the-century children had more time for play than their ancestors did. These children no doubt had work to do around their homes, but their work was probably less important to their family's survival than it might have been during the days of Aurora's pioneers.

Cyclists posed at the Aurora Public School, c.1895

Bicycling became one of Canada's favourite pastimes in the 1890s, particularly among young people who now could use their bicycles to travel far away from the watchful gaze of their elders. Some proclaimed the bicycling craze to be immoral, although this group of young people posed outside the Aurora Public School seem to be most proper.

Aurora baseball team, 1902

Second from the right in the middle row is the Rev. Edwin Pearson, Methodist minister in Aurora from 1900 to 1903 and the father of Lester ("Mike") Pearson. The Pearsons lived in the old parsonage on the southwest corner of Catherine and Spruce streets. When given a copy of this picture many years later, Mike Pearson recalled how his lifelong interest in baseball began when his father started playing in the Aurora Town Park.

Aurora lacrosse team, c.1910

Posed at the Newmarket Fair Grounds, probably just before or just after a game with Aurora's favourite rival, these young men recall a time when Canada's national sport was widely played and enjoyed.

Aurora Tennis Club, 1911

Like bicycling, lawn tennis became a popular sport in the 1890s. When the Aurora Tennis Club was formed, players began using a court set out on the north lawn of Hillary House. Clothing which today's players would find confining and restrictive was the rule of the day. Games were followed by cups of tea served from a polished brass urn.

Pool room, 1911

Less elegant than the tennis lawn at Hillary House was the pool room up above the Starland movie theatre. Many feared that pool rooms would bring idleness and corruption to Aurora's youth. But the same was said about the silent movie theatre downstairs.

Both pool room and movie theatre are gone; however, the building that housed them survives. Located on the north side of Wellington Street, just east of Yonge, the Starland has recently been extensively renovated after years of use as a general store, IGA supermarket, and Home Hardware store.

Toronto Hunt Club at Hazelburn Farm, Yonge Street, October 1923

In October 1923 Æmilius Jarvis opened his estate, Hazelburn Farm, at the south end of Aurora, to the Toronto Hunt Club. Impressed by the gently rolling countryside, the Club purchased Beverley Farm, just south of Hazelburn, in 1924. In 1922, Aurora's first horse show had been held at Hazelburn.

Both the Hunt Club and the horse show recognized the growing numbers of horse farms and hunting and show-jumping enthusiasts in this part of Ontario. Today, the Hunt Club lands are being redeveloped as a golf course and condominium housing project. The Aurora Horse Show, sponsored by the Aurora Agricultural Society, continues as a popular annual event.

Aurora Highlands Golf Club, 1945

Golf came to Aurora in 1931 with the opening of the Aurora Golf and Country Club. When this picture was taken, in 1945, a farmhouse on the site was still being used for a clubhouse. Earlier that year, the course had been purchased by Aurora Greenhouse owner Colin Nisbet, and renamed Aurora Highlands. Today, with new club facilities, surrounded by houses and condominiums, Aurora Highlands continues, testimony to the lure of the little white ball.

Aurora Lions hockey team, 1946

After World War II, hockey took over from lacrosse as one of Aurora's, and Canada's, all-time favourite sports. When it wasn't being played on the outdoor rink at the Town Park, it swung into action at the Aurora Arena.

Aurora's first indoor skating rink was built on Machell Avenue in 1885. In 1913 an arena was built next to Tannery Creek, on Yonge south of Church Street. After the roof collapsed in 1929, a new arena was built on the same site, only to be destroyed by fire one cold night in February 1965. In 1967, the Aurora Community Centre arena was built on Aurora Heights Drive.

The Temple of Fame

Women, famous in the world's history summoned by the Goddess of Fame, will plead their respective merits entitling them to the Crown

CAST OF CHARACTERS

GODDESS OF FAME .... Mrs. Charles Bilbrough

SUPPLIANTS FOR THE CROWN

1—Queen Elizabeth of England .... Miss P. Cook
2—Albani .... Mrs. J. D. Wilcox
3—Hypatia .... Miss A. Jenkins
4—Red Cross Nurse .... Miss G. Towns
5—Mary Queen of Scots .... Miss M. Warren
6—Bridget O'Flannigan .... Miss N. A. Williams
7—Madame Nordica .... Miss M. Willis
8—Queen Isabella of Spain .... Miss J. Fletcher
9—Harriet Beecher Stowe (and Topsy) .... Mrs. M. A. Andrews
10—Queen Victoria of England .... Mrs. F. D. Waite
11—Martha Washington .... Miss E. McBride
12—Marie Antoinette, Queen of France .... Miss Ina Richardson
13—Miriam (and maidens) .... Miss E. Griffiths
14—Helen of Troy .... Miss B. Hillary
15—Mrs. Partington (and Ike) .... Mrs. N. E. Eade
16—Laura Secord .... Miss M. Soanes
17—A Mother .... Mrs. R. M. Hillary
18—Cleopartra .... Miss C. McConnell
19—Maggie Mucklebackit .... Mrs. G. Reynolds
20—Joan of Arc .... Miss H. A. Griffiths
21—Josiah Allen's Wife .... Mrs. D. J. Webster
22—Francis Willard .... Mrs. A. Murray
23—Flora MacDonald .... Miss G. Pratt
24—Mother Goose (with Little Miss Muffett and Georgie Porgie .. Mrs. C. Clarke
25—Pocohontas .... Miss B. Taylor
26—Elizabeth Barrett Browning .... Miss J. Lennox
27—Ruth .... Miss W. Reynolds
28—Tabitha Primrose .... Miss H. Nelson
29—Portia .... Miss M. Stubbs
30—Madame Patti .... Miss L. Boynton
31—Sister of Charity .... Miss D. Hillary
32—Woman of the next Century .... Miss G. Petch
33—Canada .... Mrs. Charles Webster

Crown Bearers' Chorus
HAIL TO THE QUEEN

Musical Directors .... Misses B. Sisman and M. Willis

Herald .... Mr. J. G. McDonald

Guards, Pages and Attendants

Management .... Mrs. Charles Webster and Mrs. Ford Butler.

GOD SAVE THE KING

"The Temple of Fame", pageant presented at Mechanics' Hall, 1918

The Temple of Fame, "a pageant of famous women," was presented in 1918 to raise money for the overseas work of the Canadian Red Cross. Featuring local talent, it found an enthusiastic audience at Aurora's Mechanics' Hall, now the Lions Club hall, at the southeast corner of Mosley and Victoria streets.

The hall was built about 1870 and since then has seen countless meetings, auction sales, lectures, dances, plays, and concerts. It was originally owned by the Aurora branch of the Mechanics' Institute, an organization started in England to advance the education of "mechanics" — as all craftsmen, tradesmen, and factory workers were called at that time. Because of its educational goals, the Mechanics' Institute opened Aurora's first public library. The Temple of Fame was one of many events at the Mechanics' Hall that combined both entertainment and uplift.

Program for "The Temple of Fame", 1918

Marshall Forsyth's music store, east side of Yonge, just south of Wellington Street

Marshall Forsyth's store opened at least as early as 1888, selling stationery, music books, musical instruments, and sewing machines to his Aurora clientele. By the time this picture was taken, around 1910, Forsyth also was selling phonograph records.

Marshall Forsyth was part of a talented musical family. His brother Wesley was a teacher and composer who had studied in Leipzig and Vienna.

Aurora Brass Band, c.1915

In the days before phonograph records, radios, and television, Aurora had many instrumental groups. The Aurora Brass Band probably had the longest history; however, there were also the Aurora Orchestra, led by Dr. Hillary, the Aurora Saxe-Horn Band, the Fire Brigade Band, the Salvation Army Band, and the 12th Battalion Band.

In an editorial titled "A Little Too Much Music" the *Aurora Banner* of 18 April 1873 declared,

> It is said that "music hath charms to soothe the savage breast," but the extent to which this was carried last Tuesday night by the bands trying to see which could play the longest and loudest, would have a contra effect and make some calm breast savage; it caused at least one citizen to empty a basin of water from a balcony upon them, but unfortunately an unoffending individual received the contents. The

gentlemen who compose the Bands should remember that there are some invalids in our village who are made much worse by such a noise, especially when it is continued until such a late hour in the night.

The following week, however, the *Banner* reported,

The lady who threw the basin of water from the balcony the evening the Bands were playing, and to which we referred last week, wishes us to say that the water was intended for the boys who congregate there, and not for the members of the Bands, as she is very fond of their music and wishes them every success.

Band members from 1915 were, from left to right:

Back row: Harry Gray, Roy De La Haye, Ken Forsyth, George Holman, Gordon Osborne, Gordon Seaton, William Manell, Sid Davies, George Lavelle, Tom Griffith, Bob White.
Front row: Charles Boynton, Ben Davis, Harry Waterfall, Fred Luxton.

Frank Cummer at the organ in his Spruce Street art gallery, c.1930

On the back of this picture are the words "Frank Cummer, Keeper of Aurora's little Louvre." While this was something of an exaggeration, Professor Cummer was known to a generation of Aurorans as the keeper of a large collection of prints and original works of art, which he displayed in the skylit art gallery of his Spruce Street home.

Aurora Public Library craft class, 1940s

When this picture was taken, the Aurora Public Library occupied the second floor of the old Town Hall at Yonge and Mosley streets. Soon it would move a block east to Victoria Hall, which had been built as a Disciples of Christ church in 1883. In 1963, the library moved to its first permanent home on Victoria Street.

On the left is Marjorie Andrews, who served as librarian from 1934 to 1972. Thousands of Aurorans, children and adults, richly benefitted from her love of books and travel. In the centre of the photograph is Mrs. Willingham; Miss Bernice Charles is seated at the right.

*New Connexion Methodist Church
(built 1856-57), Mosley Street*

In 1847, several members of the Methodist Church at Yonge and Tyler streets broke away to join the Canadian Wesleyan Methodist New Connexion Church and opened their own church on Temperance Street, less than a block away. In 1856, these same Methodists acquired land on the north side of Mosley Street and built this substantial building shortly thereafter. When the two Methodist groups reunited in 1875, this church was sold to the Primitive Methodists. In 1885, the Primitive Methodists sold it to the Salvation Army who continued to use the building until 1972. It now serves as a child care centre.

Aurora's oldest church building, the New Connexion Methodist church combines both classical and Gothic Revival motifs.

Its bold pediment and brick pilasters suggest the outline of a Greek temple, while its tall pointed windows capped by wooden drip mouldings bring to mind the Gothic style. These windows were altered after the church was turned into a day-care centre. Similarities to Willowdale Presbyterian Church, St. John's Church at York Mills, and Christ Church in Holland Landing suggest that this too is the work of Toronto architect and philanthropist John Howard.

Immediately to the right of the church in this photograph is a corner of the Italianate-style Baldwin house. Built by James Andrews sometime between 1875 and 1877, it has been in the Baldwin family since 1889.

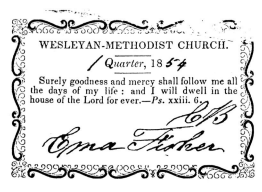

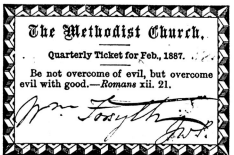

*Methodist communion cards,
1854 and 1887*

*Methodist Church Sunday School class,
c.1874*

The Methodists, like many other Protestant denominations, used printed cards to admit church members to communion services and to keep track of those who attended. These cards probably represent services which were missed, otherwise their holders would have handed them in. In any case, these two cards were considered important enough to have been put away carefully with family papers for many years.

Methodists built Aurora's first church in 1818, although no doubt Methodist meetings were held in local barns and farmhouses long before that.

This is the only glimpse we have of the old frame church which stood at the north corner of Yonge and Tyler streets. It had been built in 1855 to replace an earlier log meeting house on land donated to the Methodists by William Tyler, a United Empire Loyalist who had come to the Yonge Street settlement in 1799 after first trying his luck in New Brunswick.

Methodist Church (built 1878), Yonge and Tyler streets

After fire damaged the old frame church in March 1877, its congregation decided to build a new and much larger building. The editor of the *Banner* wrote on April 20, "The site is a very prominent one and a large and beautiful church would not only add vastly to the appearance of the village, but be more in keeping with the wealth and respectability of the congregation." The Toronto firm of Henry Langley, one of Canada's most prominent church architects, was hired to design this building. Including furnishings, it cost $12,130 — a substantial sum at a time when few workingmen earned over a dollar a day. The new church was designed in the popular Gothic Revival style. Its taller steeple rose 146 feet in the air, a soaring testament of faith. Sadly, both steeples were damaged in a cyclone which struck Aurora only fifteen years later. They were rebuilt, but only to a fraction of their original height. More sadly still, even these shorter spires were eventually removed, leaving only their supporting towers behind.

Looking west on Mosley Street toward the Methodist church, c.1900

Mosley Street was aligned so that the Methodist (now Aurora United) church would be at its head. How beautiful was the vista toward the church, even with its shortened spires! How graceful were the trees and boulevards before traffic, heavy wires, and hydro poles began to take their toll.

Methodist Church interior, c.1900

Its walls painted with flowing leaves and vines, framing an elaborate display of false organ pipes, the interior of the Aurora Methodist Church was a far cry from the barns and simple meeting houses visited in days of old by the travelling circuit riders and saddlebag preachers who had brought Methodism to the Canadian frontier.

NINE CENT SALE

Wednesday October the Ninth, 1907, by the W.M.S. of the Methodist Church, Aurora.

On the NINTH, without fail,
Will be held the noted NINE Cent Sale,
By the tireless ladies of the Methodist Band,
Who not for one moment fatigue would stand.

The doors of the basement will be open wide,
And for NINE Cents you may go inside,
And every lucky NINTH one
May go in free and see the fun.

There'll be bargain packages piled up high,
And NINE round cents your choice can buy
Each one warranted to contain
NINE Cents worth of certain gain.

You can eat ice cream for NINE Cents,
So good you'll forget all about expense,
And for fancy work you'll find a few,
At prices that end in NINE or so.

It may be a great surprise to you,
To hear what things they have planned to do :
At four o'clock you'll want to see
NINE Auxiliary ladies serving tea.

These ladies carry neither firearm nor gun,
But they give you the cup when the tea is done :
Yes, the saucer, too, and you'll want to own
So pretty an addition to your tea-table home.

At last, when your money is fully gone,
You hate to leave the social throng,
You'll hear just a whisper of exquisite sound,
So faint, yet so true, such tones full and round.

That you turn to your neighbor who at once sets you
straight,
By saying : "Don't you know it is eight
The time for the concert, the treat for us all,
And then do you that hour recall ?"

So remember everyone, I pray,
At four o'clock on the NINTH day
Of the present month, come wet or dry,
Please gather to eat and talk and buy.

Mrs. Stevenson's Excelsior Bible Class, Aurora Methodist Church, 1910

Only a strong and determined woman such as Mrs. William Stevenson, shown here front row centre, could have led a large all-male Bible study class such as this one.

When not leading Bible classes or teaching Sunday School, Mrs. Stevenson was an accomplished artist, painting the walls of the church parlour with roses, and teaching young ladies the popular art of china painting.

From left to right are:

Front row: F. Bush, J. Anderson, J.J. Hill, W. Madden, Mrs. Stevenson, Rev. C. Dobson, F. Anderson, C. Bilbrough, W. Tight.
Second row: H. Dobson, W. Sullivan, I. Clubine, R. Hacking, H. Strasler, R. De La Haye, unknown, W. Steadman, F.E. York.
Third row: H. Manning, E. Bradbury, B. Andrews, M. Graham, H. Cosford, W. Briggs, W. Sisman, H. Grimshaw, T. Graham.
Back row: O. Brett, E. Davis, C. Ney, F. MacIntyre, Mr. Tilson.

Trinity Anglican Church (built 1846) and rectory (built 1862), Victoria and Metcalfe streets

Church of England services were first recorded in Aurora in September 1843 at the home of John Mosley, on Yonge Street. Shortly afterwards plans were made to build a church on land donated by Mr. Mosley. The church shown in this photograph was built in 1846 and is attributed to architect Thomas Harris. In 1857/58, a large brick and stone addition was made to the original frame building. In 1862, a brick rectory was built to the northeast.

The church was located so that it could easily be seen from Yonge Street, standing at the top of a hill at the head of Church Street. Appropriate to the Anglican Church's ties to colonial government, that site was also at the corner of Victoria and Metcalfe streets, streets named after the reigning monarch and the colonial governor of the time.

Before the village had its own bell, Simon Appleton was appointed by village by-law to ring the Trinity Church bell in case of fire or other emergency.

Interior of 1846 Trinity Church

This interior view of the 1846 Trinity Anglican Church was taken after the 1858 brick and stone addition had been built. This addition made the church cruciform in shape, providing wide transcepts on either side of the chancel area.

Still, it was a rather plain building, little influenced by the Ecclesiological Movement or the "high church" Gothic revival which then was gathering momentum.

To the right of the chancel is a small pipe organ installed in 1872. It once had been used at St. James Cathedral in Toronto.

Interior of 1883 Trinity Anglican Church

Decorated for a "Harvest Home" service in November 1893, this is the interior of the present Trinity Anglican Church designed in 1883 by architect Marshall B. Aylesworth. Its deep chancel, stained glass, and richly patterned walls and ceilings are in striking contrast to the plainness of the 1846 church it replaced. Overhead are large gasoliers, replaced by electric lighting in 1917.

St. Andrew's Presbyterian Church (built 1873), northeast corner of Mosley and Victoria streets

St. Andrew's Presbyterian Church used a combination of red and buff brick popular in Ontario's late Victorian architecture. It originally had a steeple, but this was destroyed by the cyclone of 1893.

Among the fund-raising events held to build this church was a peach festival duly recorded by the *Aurora Banner* in September 1872. Consuming plates of oysters, peaches, and ice cream to the music of the Fire Brigade Band, the Presbyterians ate their way to a $300 profit.

Presbyterian services began in Aurora in 1871. While the church was badly divided over union with the Methodists in 1925, it continued to grow and prosper until expansion forced the demolition of the original church building in 1963. Fortunately, the round stained-glass window shown here on the façade was saved from destruction and reinstalled in St. Andrew's Hall behind the new church building.

Wellington Street Regular Baptist Church (built 1883), west corner of Wellington and Victoria streets

Like St. Andrew's one block to the south, the Wellington Street Regular Baptist Church, now known as First Baptist Church, was a simple Gothic Revival structure with pointed lancet windows and heavy brick buttresses. And like St. Andrew's, it proved to be too small to house its growing congregation in the early 1960s.

Like many Aurora buildings of its time, it was built of buff-coloured brick made in a brickyard at the foot of Reuben Street, behind present-day George Street School. Even today one can see where yellow clay was taken from the side of the hill there to make bricks. In a demonstration of ecumenical good will, some of the bricks from this Baptist church were used to face the 1964 narthex addition at Trinity Anglican Church, perfectly blending the new and the old.

Interior of Aurora Gospel Church, Yonge Street, 1940s

From this picture of the Aurora Gospel Church decorated for a Thanksgiving service in the 1940s, one could hardly imagine that this had once been the Pine Orchard Friends Meeting House, said to have been built prior to 1809. The Pine Orchard Friends (Quakers) were located in Whitchurch township, east of Newmarket. Their meeting house, unneeded after the present Pine Orchard Union Church was built next door, was sold to the Gospel Church and moved to the west side of Yonge Street in Aurora, just south of Church Street, in 1945. A few years after this picture was taken, the Gospel Church moved to the old Mechanics' Hall at Mosley and Victoria streets and the old meeting house was turned over to commercial use. Today, a lighting store is located there.

Our Lady of Grace Roman Catholic Church (built 1953), Yonge Street

Roman Catholic services first were held in Aurora at De La Salle College near Yonge Street and Bloomington Road. In 1949, *Inglehurst*, the old Fleury estate, was acquired by the diocese. No doubt this met with the full approval of H.W. Fleury's daughter, Marguerite, who had left Aurora to live in France and there converted to Roman Catholicism.

For a while, services were held in the old Fleury house itself. In 1953, this simple Georgian Revival-style church was built, leaving the house as a rectory and a residence for some of the teachers at Our Lady of Grace School, just to the east.

In 1983, a growing parish forced the demolition of this building and the erection of a much larger church on the same site.

Handbill advertising an elocutionary contest sponsored by the Royal Templars of Temperance, 1897

This contest was sponsored by one of the several temperance organizations which were found in Aurora in the nineteenth century. The first such organization, Whitchurch Division No.106, Sons of Temperance, was chartered in 1850 and built its own hall on the west side of Temperance Street, between Wellington and Tyler streets.

The temperance movement sought to curb excessive drinking at a time when Canadian men, women, and children drank astonishing amounts of hard liquor. Alcoholism was a major problem in pioneer society, a problem made worse by Aurora's several hotels and bar rooms. Village by-law number two, passed in 1863, permitted bar rooms to open at 5:00 a.m. They had to close at 11:00 every night but Saturday — when they closed at 7:00 — and were kept closed all day Sunday. The Sunday closing law was not always obeyed, however.

Miss Eva Petch was the winner of this contest in 1897.

SILVER MEDAL

An Elocutionary Contest for a Silver Medal will be held in the

LECTURE ROOM
—OF THE—

METHODIST CHURCH,
—ON—

Wed. Eve., April 28,

Under the Auspices of Aurora Council, Royal Templars of Temperance.

PROGRAMME:

1. Opening Ode......   ....
2. Chairman's Speech....   ....
3. Contestant No. 1....   ....
4. Instrumental duet....   ....   ..Misses Dicker and Hill.
5. Contestant No. 2....   ....
6. Duet.. ....Mr. and Mrs. Reynolds.
7. Contestant No. 3....   ....
8. Instrumental Trio.....   ....Misses Querrie.
9. Contestant No. 4......   ....
10. Selection......   ....Aurora Glee Club.
11. Contestant No 5....   ....
12. Instrumental Duet....   ....Miss Scott & Master Reynolds.
13. Contestant No. 6....   ....
14. Cartoon....   ....Mr. C. Stone.
15. Contestant No. 7....   ....
16. Song....   ....Rev. T. Dunlop.
17. Contestant No. 8..   ....
18. Selection......   ....Aurora Glee Club.
19. Contestant No. 9..   ....
20. Speech....   ....J. M. Walton, G.W.P., S. of T.
21. Speech   ....J. S. Green, District Councillor.
22. Speech....   ....Rev. H. S. Matthews, Dom. Chaplain.
23. Decision of Judges and awarding the Medal....   ....

JUDGES:
L. Rush, B.A.;   W. Megill, B.A;   Rev. M. Chapman, B.A.

Hon. E. J. DAVIS
Will occupy the chair.

ADMISSION: -   -   10 CTS-

DOORS OPEN AT 7.30.   COMMENCE AT 8 O'CLOCK SHARP.

Interior of Rising Sun Masonic lodge (built 1877), Mosley and Wells streets

Like the Sons of Temperance, the Masons were another organization which could be found in nearly every pioneer community. In Aurora, the Rising Sun Masonic lodge was chartered in 1860. In 1885, the Masons bought this building at the southwest corner of Mosley and Wells streets. Their old hall, built c.1866 at Centre Street and what is now called Walton Drive, was moved about 1897 to Victoria Street to be used by Trinity Anglican Church as a parish hall. The Masons' new home, at Mosley and Wells, had been built by the Methodist Episcopal Church in 1877.

The hall's interior is remarkable in that it has changed relatively little since the time when this picture was taken about 1906. Its walls are rich with Masonic symbols painted by Mrs. William Stevenson.

The Maccabees, like the Masons and the Oddfellows, were an organization which traced its roots far back in time. They were known for their charitable work as well as their ritual and offered insurance schemes and savings plans to their members long before the days of government-supported programs. Judging from this picture, the Maccabees also may have provided a necessary social outlet for their members, allowing men who may have felt the restraints of Victorian propriety by day to dress up in costume at lodge meetings by night. While the Masons and the Oddfellows still play an active role in Aurora today, the Maccabees have long faded from memory, despite their costumes.

Orange parade, 12 July, 1930s, Yonge and Mosley streets

The Orange lodge drew its members from people of Protestant background who paraded behind "King Billy," King William of Orange, every 12th of July, the anniversary of the Battle of the Boyne, when Protestant forces defeated the Catholics in northern Ireland.

The Aurora lodge gained notoriety in 1860 during a brief visit by the Prince of Wales. Wanting to maintain the good will of Canada's Catholic population, the Prince wished to avoid any association with the Orangemen. The ingenious Orangemen of Aurora, however, erected a large arch right over the railway line where the Prince's train would travel. Quoting from *The Prince of Wales in Canada and the United States*, published in 1861:

At most of the little villages there were arches; at

112

Aurora there were three erected right across the line. One was simple and pretty; another was Masonic and unintelligible; the third was Orange. There was no mistake about the character of this last. It was pure Orange, with all its insignia — the portrait of the "glorious, pious, and immortal Monarch," and the letters and number of the lodge by which it was stuck up. It was right across the line, too, so there was no help for it or time to help it, and the royal train with the Prince, per force, passed under the Orange arch. No one in it could forbear a smile at the obstinate pertinacity displayed by the Orangemen, and the ingenious manner in which they had compelled His Royal Highness to pass under their party emblem, all bedizened as it was with the most obnoxious of their banners.

Aurora Lions Club Ladies' Night, Lake Simcoe Hotel, late 1940s

Since 1944, the Lions Club has been one of Aurora's most active organizations, raising money for charity, boosting community spirit, and generally helping out wherever there is need. Here, however, the occasion was strictly for fun: "Ladies' Night" at the Lake Simcoe Hotel, a popular summertime destination for dancing and a night out.

Boy Scouts parade float, 1949

A Boy Scout troop was first established in Aurora at Trinity Anglican Church in 1914.

This picture shows an ambitious Boy Scout float driven in an Aurora parade by Billy Calhoun. On the wagon lent by Aurora Orchards are Garry Knowles, Robin Noble, Jack Brooks, Peter Hodgkinson, Bob Murby, and Don Hooper.

Ted Rothwell's harness shop, c.1915

Getting around in early Aurora meant travelling by foot or by horse. While this picture was not taken until after the turn of the century, harness making, repairing, and selling were among Aurora's earliest and most necessary trades.

Grand Trunk Railway station (built 1900), Wellington Street East

Ontario, Simcoe & Huron Railroad ticket, c.1855

The coming of the railway brought dramatic change to the village, ending years of isolation. Regular stagecoach service had existed on Yonge Street since 1828, but it was the railway that made travel easy and enjoyable for the first time.

This ticket was issued by the Ontario, Simcoe & Huron Union Railroad, which opened Ontario's first railway from Toronto to Machell's Corners on 16 May 1853. Later that year, service was extended to Newmarket. In 1855, it opened to Collingwood, providing a direct link with the steamships that plied the upper Great Lakes. A provincial plaque on the grounds of the Aurora railway station marks this historic line.

Aurora's first railway station, served by the Ontario, Simcoe & Huron railway and later the Northern Railway, was built on or close to this site. An insurance map for 1885, however, shows a depot on the west side of the railway tracks. In 1900, the line was operated by the Grand Trunk Railway which built this station according to one of their standard designs. This postcard view shows the station in its heyday, with board-and-batten siding and carefully tended grounds that made it a fitting gateway to Aurora for weary travellers.

Across the tracks, at Wellington and Berczy streets, stood the Wellington Hotel. Just to the north was the Railroad Hotel, which stands today as a private residence.

This old station survives as well, serving commuters every weekday. Its past glory has faded and its walls are covered with "insulbrick," but hopes for its restoration still run high.

Royal Hotel, east side Yonge Street, c.1890

Queen's Hotel, northeast corner of Yonge and Wellington streets, c.1900

Aurora boasted several hotels at a time when travel from place to place could still be difficult and time-consuming and when commercial travellers needed places to stay and to set up their wares. George Lemon ran this hotel near the corner of Yonge and Mosley streets. Previously he had operated the Yonge Street Hotel and the Aurora Hotel nearby. Novelist Mazo de la Roche, George Lemon's niece, often visited here as a girl and used a description of this hotel in one of her *Jalna* novels.

The Queen's, built around 1860 as The Machell House, was Aurora's largest and most elegant hotel. On its roof was a handsome belvedere which gave light to a gracefully curving stairway three storeys below. In order to lure travellers from the station, a horse-drawn omnibus met every train. In 1878, the Queen's, like George Lemon's hotel, became a temperance house, making up for the loss of revenue at its bar by charging higher prices for meals and for the use of its stables. Among its regular guests was the travelling phrenologist, Mark Mendleson, who examined the shape of his clients' heads in order to assess their talents and personalities.

The Queen's survived until 1971, a mere shadow of its former glory, when it was demolished to make way for the Toronto Dominion Bank. One cannot help but regret the fact that the bank was unable to renovate this fine old building instead of building anew.

Laying the radial railway tracks, Yonge Street, 1899

Radial railway station (built 1906), Yonge Street

Here workmen are laying track for the Metropolitan Radial Railway, an electric streetcar line which eventually would stretch from Toronto north to Lake Simcoe. A branch line, the Schomberg & Aurora Railway, linked Schomberg and Oak Ridges. The Metropolitan carried passengers, freight, and mail. It made travel up and down Yonge Street easier than ever before and helped usher in a new era of commuters and suburbs.

This picture was taken in front of *Horton Place*, just north of the corner of Yonge Street and Irwin Avenue. At the opposite side of the road is *Castle Doan*.

This station stood just north of the Methodist (now United) Church and was enlarged to two storeys in 1912. After the radial line closed in 1930, the building was turned around and used as a gas station.

Radial railway car, 1912

From left to right in this photograph taken in 1912 are Metropolitan employees Dutch Schmidt, Bill Ellison, and Harry Holman.

Bond Lake,
Ont Canada.

Radial cars at Bond Lake, c.1914

Excursions by radial car to Bond Lake, just south of Aurora, were favourite summer pastimes. There the company operated a spacious park and a picnic pavilion. There too were the company's generating station and repair barns.

De La Haye service station and blacksmith shop, Yonge Street, c.1935

Roy De La Haye's Supertest gas station and blacksmith shop on the west side of Yonge Street, between Wellington Street and Irwin Avenue, stood at the crossroads of two eras in Aurora's history. Some farmers in the area still used horses around their farms and needed the services of a blacksmith both to shoe their horses and to repair their implements. But this was also the beginning of the automobile age. Soon large gas stations with bright lights and large electric signs would come to dominate parts of a street which once had known only the sounds of horses' hoofs, creaking wagons and carriages, and whirring electric trolley cars.

Car parked on Yonge Street, 1948

It was in 1948 when this streamlined automobile parked in front of the Aurora municipal offices on the east side of Yonge Street. The automobile had brought the brief era of the radial cars to an end in 1930. By then more people had private cars for travel up and down Yonge Street and diesel-powered buses seemed more comfortable and convenient. Also, the radial cars and their tracks seemed always to be in the way.

121

*Poster advertising Queen's birthday
celebrations, 24 May 1861*

Mock battles, church services, torchlight processions, fireworks, games, and races — all were part of traditional celebrations of holidays such as Queen Victoria's birthday.

Procession on Yonge Street, 1890s

This photograph was taken from the roof of *Inglehurst*, the Fleury residence, looking south onto Yonge Street. In the left foreground are *Castle Doan* and a three-gabled house on Catherine Avenue. Flags are flying high in the background, while two white banners have been stretched across Yonge Street.

The occasion being celebrated is not known; however, it may have been in honour of Queen Victoria's Diamond Jubilee in 1897.

Old Boys and Girls Reunion Committee, July 1914

In that last summer of peace before the Great War, Aurora held a reunion, attracting between four and five thousand people at a time when the town's entire population was less than two thousand. From the first to the third of July, townsfolk and their guests enjoyed a "huge calithumpian procession," concerts, sports, tableaux, fireworks, and a military tattoo.

These rather sober-looking gentlemen were part of the organizing committee.

Santa Claus Parade, 1913

On 14 November 1913 Santa Claus came to Aurora on a float featuring live reindeer. He was part of an Eaton's Santa Claus Parade which started in Newmarket and made its way down Yonge Street to Toronto.

Post Office decorated for Canada's diamond jubilee, 1927

Public buildings draped with flags and bunting have long been traditional symbols of celebration. Here the Aurora post office is decked out in honour of Canada's Diamond Jubilee, the 60th anniversary of Confederation, in 1927.

Coronation parade float, 12 May 1937

Just as Canada was beginning to pull out of a long period of depression and at a time when loyalty to the motherland still ranked high, this was one of many floats in Aurora's Coronation Day parade in honour of King George VI and Queen Elizabeth. This float was sponsored by Sisman's shoe company and was photographed in front of the Sisman factory on Berczy Street.

From left to right are Robert Bull dressed as an Eskimo, Cecil Holman as a Mountie, F. Griffith as a farmer, Harry Burge as an Indian, and J. Morton as an industrial labourer.

125

Santa Claus and a group of excited children, late 1940s

Here Santa Claus is meeting with an excited group of youngsters on Yonge Street downtown. In the background is a glimpse of Aurora's elaborate Christmas lighting. From 1946 until the mid-sixties, Aurora was known far and wide for its colourful lights installed under the direction of hydro manager Charles Copland. Strings of coloured lights, stars, and scrolls were hung across Yonge and Wellington streets from one end of the town to the other. At the Yonge and Wellington intersection, a huge lighted bell heralded the arrival of each Christmas season.

Members of the 127th Battalion (York Rangers) gathering at Town Park, April 1916

Shortly after this picture was taken, members of the 127th Battalion would join ranks and march west to Yonge Street. There they would climb onto the radial cars to go to Kodak Barracks at Mount Dennis. After several weeks of training, they would be off to Europe and the horrors of World War I. In the foreground is Surgeon Lieutenant-Colonel Robert Michael Hillary on his horse, Dolly. To the right is the old Aurora Armoury built in 1872.

The Armoury is now home to "A" Squadron of the Queen's York Rangers, Canada's oldest regiment. The Armoury itself is one of the oldest in Canada still in military use.

RED CROSS TEA GROUNDS
"INGLEHURST"
AURORA - ONTARIO

*Red Cross tea at "Inglehurst",
September 1915*

During World War I, the spacious grounds of *Inglehurst*, the H.W. Fleury house on Yonge Street, were used for fund-raising teas by the Aurora branch of the Red Cross.

128

Water Tower Park with German cannon in place, 1920s

Cenotaph, 1925

In 1920, the Director of War Trophies wrote to Aurora Council to say that the town had been offered a German cannon. In a sense, this became Aurora's first World War I memorial. It was placed on a concrete platform near Yonge Street in front of the old waterworks. In 1956, the cannon was located in front of the Legion hall on Yonge Street. Its current whereabouts are unknown.

Shown here is the memorial tower which stands proudly on Yonge Street at the south end of Aurora. It was built to recognize all those from Aurora, King, and Whitchurch who served and died during the Great War.

Appropriately, it was constructed on land which once had belonged to military leader William Graham. Graham had fought for the British during the American Revolution. He also served as colonel of the 1st Regiment of York Militia during the War of 1812.

Dedication of "Altar of Sacrifice" at the Cenotaph

This "Altar of Sacrifice" was dedicated in 1960 to commemorate those who had died during the Second World War. Assisting in the ceremony were Mrs. Cecil Walker, Lieutenant-Governor J. Keiller Mackay, and aide-de-camp (and future Aurora mayor) Dick Illingworth.

Legion hall under construction, late 1940s

Following the Second World War, the Aurora branch of the Royal Canadian Legion built this hall near the north corner of Yonge Street and Dunning Avenue. It served as a popular local meeting place until 1974, when the present Legion hall was built on Industrial Parkway North.

At the time of the move to the new hall, the Aurora branch was named after Colonel Fred Tilston, VC, who served in the Canadian armed forces from 1940 to 1945 and took part in both the Normandy invasion and the campaign into Germany. Tilston was president of Sterling Drug from 1957 to 1971.

View from Temperance Street hill following cyclone of 1893

On May 23, 1893, a cyclone tore through Aurora leaving this scene of devastation. Part of the tall steeple of the Aurora Methodist (now United) Church lies on the south side of Tyler Street. Windows on the south side of the church, along with windows at the Town Hall at Mosley and Yonge streets, have been smashed.

The cyclone hit town from the southwest, demolishing the judges' stand, barn, and fences at the Driving Park. It then tore off a barn roof and severely damaged several houses on Kennedy Street before bearing down toward Yonge Street. At Tyler and Yonge it struck both the Methodist Church and the Town Hall and badly injured James Reynolds, whose horse and rig were blown across Yonge Street. The storm continued eastward, flattening the Salvation Army sheds and lifting the steeple off the Presbyterian Church. It destroyed the southeast corner of the Stevenson house at the corner of Wellington and Wells streets, leaving bedrooms exposed to the street but most of the windows and the roof undamaged.

House on Temperance Street after the flood of 1946

Heavy rains led to severe flooding in low-lying areas of Aurora in the summer of 1946. Here, this house on the east side of Temperance Street was hard hit when Tannery Creek overflowed its banks — although these children seem to be enjoying themselves just the same. An even worse storm followed in 1954 when Hurricane Hazel hit town.

Jesse M. Walton and Sir William Mulock, Aurora Town Park, July 1914

Both of these men were prominent local politicians and Liberal party workers. Sir William Mulock, on the right, lived on a country estate still owned by his descendants, just north of Aurora. He served as Member of Parliament from 1882 to 1905 and as postmaster-general and first minister of labour in the government of Sir Wilfrid Laurier. He was chief justice of Ontario from 1923 to 1936 and served as chancellor of the University of Toronto until his death at age 100 in 1944.

J.M. Walton was mayor of Aurora from 1923 to 1928 and again in 1939-40. On several occasions he ran unsuccessfully for provincial parliament. Walton had a passionate interest in local history and genealogy. He established his own private museum at his summer home in Kettleby and in 1936 began gathering local artifacts for display in the Aurora post office. Walton's collection forms the nucleus of the Aurora Museum's collection today.

T. Herbert Lennox

William Lyon Mackenzie King, from a 1921 campaign postcard

"Herb" Lennox, who lived in the large white stuccoed house which stands near the northwest corner of Wells and Metcalfe streets, served as an Aurora town councillor for three terms, and as Member of Provincial Parliament for North York from 1905 to 1919. In 1925 he entered federal politics and defeated Prime Minister William Lyon Mackenzie King for a seat in Ottawa. He continued as a federal member of Parliament until his death in 1934. The "Lennox Picnic," held every summer from 1905 to 1934 at Jackson's Point, was a popular occasion for hundreds of his supporters.

Lennox was a consummate politician, rarely rising in the house to speak on any matter, but always eager to listen to the concerns of his constituents.

Mackenzie King ran unsuccessfully for Member of Parliament for North York in 1917. He ran for office here because of his strong sentimental ties to his grandfather, William Lyon Mackenzie, who also had represented this area and who had led his supporters in the Rebellion of 1837. King ran again in 1921, this time as leader of the Liberal Party. He won and became not only Member of Parliament for North York, but Prime Minister of Canada as well. In 1925, however, King was defeated by Conservative Herb Lennox and never chose to run in this riding again.

Aurora Village Council, 1863

In 1855, Aurora achieved the status of police village governed by three trustees, John Campbell, John T. Gurnett, and James Mosley. Local government was severely limited, however, until Aurora's incorporation as a village in 1863.

Here is the first village council. From left to right they are: Robert Boyd, George L. Stevenson, Reeve Charles Doan, Clerk Charles York, Seth Ashton, and James Holladay.

Council meetings first were held at the village's hotels. In 1864, however, council authorized the purchase of a former store at Yonge and Mosley streets to accommodate a council chamber and fire hall.

Town Hall (built 1875-76), north corner of Yonge and Mosley streets

Taken about 1950, this photograph shows the Aurora Town Hall in its last days. After a great deal of public controversy, it was begun late in 1875 according to designs by the Toronto firm of Langley, Langley, and Burke. Its ground floor contained a farmers' market at the front, with a council chamber, clerk's office, vault, fire station, and lock-up cells at the back. Upstairs was a large hall with a stage across the west end.

A letter to the *Aurora Banner* of 19 November 1875 quoted a farmer from Whitchurch who said, "I think if the Aurora folks had any gumpshon they would try and make better roads through their village before they vested their money building such fan-dangles as that Town Hall." Nevertheless, the Town Hall did become the centre of much of Aurora's business, political, and social life for eighty years.

It was demolished in 1956 at a time when few Canadians were interested in preserving the landmarks of their past. Had it survived a decade or so longer, its fate might have been different.

VILLAGE of AURORA,
~COUNTY OF YORK~

No. 412   Oct. 9 1885

Mr. Richard Pengally & Estate R. Connor

Amount of Assessment on Real Property	975
Amount of Assessment on Personal Property	
Amount of Income Assessed	
Total as Confirmed by Court of Revision	
County Rate, 8 cents in the $100	90
Village Rate, 40 cents in the $100	1 50
Industrial Home Rate, 3 cents in the $100	11
Dog Tax, $1 each	
Bitch Tax, $2 each	
School Rates, 52 cents in the $100	1 95
Total Taxes	3 86

Received Payment.

     C. A. Petch Collector.

NOTICE.

The 94th Section of the Assessment Act of 1859 enacts: That in case any party shall refuse or neglect to pay the taxes imposed upon him for the space of fourteen days after demand, the Collector shall levy the same with costs, by distress and sale of goods and chattels of the party who ought to pay the same. Also Section two of By-Law 165 enacts: That all persons so liable for taxes as aforesaid, and are in default for not having paid their municipal taxes respectively on or before the fourteenth day of December preceeding the election, each and every year hereafter, shall be excluded from the voters's list, in accordance with the statute in such case made and provided; and it shall be the duty of the Returning Officer to refuse to record the vote of each person known to him to be in default for his municipal taxes.

☞ The Collector will be at the Council Room every Wednesday and Friday afternoon from 2 to 6 o'clock, to receive taxes.

Village of Aurora tax bill, 1885

Municipal taxes were a mere $3.86 on this bill dated 9 October 1885. It is signed by tax collector Charles Albert Petch, who had been hired by the village in 1883 as Chief Constable as well as caretaker of the Town Hall and Council Chamber, Bell Ringer, Market Clerk, Fire and Nuisance Inspector, Caretaker of the Engine Room, Bookkeeper, and Lamplighter. In 1888, Petch also became Aurora's first waterworks engineer, moving with his family into the small house above the pumping station on Yonge Street south of Church Street. He continued working for Aurora for nearly forty-five years. The last twelve years of his life, C.A. Petch served as Town Clerk. He died in 1927 of pneumonia contracted while he was sorting through waterlogged papers damaged during a fire at the Town Hall.

Aurora Town Council, 1945

By the time this picture was taken, Council was meeting in the old Sterling Bank building, built about 1920 just north of the post office and purchased by the Town in 1943. Town administration had outgrown the old Town Hall and more space was needed there for the fire department. The Sterling Bank building continued as Aurora's municipal offices until 1976 when a new Administrative Centre was opened on Wellington Street West.

Here, from left to right, are Bill West, Ellwood Davis, Crawford Rose, Deputy-Reeve Asa Cook, Mayor Ross Linton, Reeve C.E. Sparks, Nixon Fisher, and Rod Smith.

Police directing traffic at Yonge and Wellington streets during Aurora centennial celebration, July 1963

Dressed up like turn-of-the-century "Keystone Cops" are Don Coombes and Jim Krochter with their portable traffic signal at the corner of Yonge and Wellington streets. The occasion was Aurora's centennial celebrations in July 1963.

In 1971, Aurora's police department became part of a much larger force serving all York Region.

Presentation of chain of office, 8 January 1963

Here former mayor Dr. Crawford Rose congratulates Mayor Keith Nisbet following the presentation of his chain of office at Aurora Council's 1963 inaugural meeting held at Dr. G.W. Williams Secondary School. The chain was produced under the direction of Rod Smith to mark Aurora's centennial of incorporation. It bears the Town of Aurora crest, the coats of arms of Canada and Ontario, and medals struck to commemorate Aurora's hundredth birthday.

This was the first of many special events held that year to mark the centennial. Although the early 1960s had been a time of massive growth and change and Aurora's population had more than doubled between 1958 and 1963, Aurora's centennial brought together old and new residents of the town in an extraordinary display of optimism and pride.

INDEX

BIBLIOGRAPHY

Primary Sources

Vital to the preparation of this book have been records and plans filed at the York Region Registry Office in Newmarket. Census records, available on microfilm at the Archives of Ontario and the Aurora Public Library, and assessment records and council minutes preserved by the Town of Aurora also have been important.

Original and microfilmed copies of the *Aurora Banner*, published since 1864, have been useful as well, as were the short-lived *Aurora Sun* from 1858 and the *Aurora Borealis* which started in 1877 as the *Liberal Conservative* and lasted until 1889.

Business directories are another important source of information, two of the most interesting being the *Aurora Trade Guide and Advertiser* (1865) and *Commercial, Industrial and Progressive . . . Newmarket, Aurora, Bradford and Richmond Hill, Ontario* (c.1917).

The research files of the Aurora Museum and the Town of Aurora Heritage Committee (LACAC) have also provided rich sources of information.

Secondary sources

Adams, Wilfred. *History of Rising Sun Lodge A.F. & A.M., No. 129, G.R.C. 1860-1960* (Aurora, 1960).

Aurora lodge No. 148, I.O.O.F. 1874-1974 (Aurora, 1974).

Baker Pearce, Jean. *A History of the Development of Electricity in Aurora* (Aurora, 1967).

Berchem, F.R. *The Yonge Street Story 1793-1860* (Toronto, 1977).

Bull, Stewart H. *The Queen's York Rangers: An Historic Regiment* (Erin, 1984).

Byers, Mary, and Jan Kennedy, Margaret McBurney, and the Junior League of Toronto. *Rural Roots: Pre-Confederation Buildings of the York Region of Ontario* (Toronto, 1976).

Commemorative Biographical Record of the County of York, Ontario (Toronto, 1907).

First Baptist Church, Aurora, Ontario, 1883-1983 (Aurora, 1983).

Johnston, James, *Aurora: Its Early Beginnings* (1963; 2nd ed. Aurora, 1972).

McIntyre, W. John and Michael, Wills, *Hillary House ("The Manor")* (Aurora, 1975).

McIntyre, W. John. *Sticks and Stones: A Story of Aurora's Municipal Buildings* (Aurora, 1976).

Mitchell, John. *The Settlement of York County* (Toronto, 1950).

Myers, Jay. *The Great Canadian Road* (Toronto, 1977).

150th Anniversary of the Founding and Dedication of Aurora United Church (Aurora, 1968).

Robinson, C. Blackett. *History of Toronto and County of York, Ontario.* 2 vols. (Toronto, 1885).

Robinson, Percy J. *Toronto During the French Régime: A History of the Toronto Region from Brûlé to Simcoe, 1615-1793* (1933; 2nd ed. Toronto, 1965).

Simpson, B. Napier, Jr. "Walking Tour of Aurora," *The York Pioneer* (1964), pp.56-61.

Stacey, C.P. "A Dream of My Youth': Mackenzie King in North York," *Ontario History*, vol. LXXVI, 273-286.

Stuart, Jacqueline. "Big Fish in a Small Pond: The Jarvises Invest in Aurora,". *The York Pioneer* (1986), pp.16-28.

Trinity Church, Aurora, 1846-1946 (Aurora, 1946).

Wickson, Ted. "The Radial Railways of North Yonge Street, Upper Canada Railway Society *Newsletter* (March/April 1973), pp. 44-58.